LAUGH WITH THE NAVY

By
Jim Swift

**This book is dedicated to my daughter
Nicola and her mum — my severest
critics!!**

We'll accept you . . . you'll make an excellent club swinger!

2

It's a pity about your dodgy eyesight . . . you'd have made an excellent Frogman!

Do you want someting to bite on?

Junior Seaman who!

Have you taken I.D. card photographs before snaps?

No you CAN'T be excused divisions. You're the Captain aren't you!

**That's right sir, all my pupils pass their swimming test
on their first attempt!**

If it fits, bring it back and we'll change it for you!

You want to learn self-defence? . . . against what?

I asked the Doc for something to make me sleep, he
handed me a copy of the Seamanship manual.

How do you expect me to read it, it's not even written in English!

**The Captain's approved your request to buy yourself out,
in fact, he'll even provide the money!**

No I'm not a sloppy dresser . . . just a sloppy eater!

**How would you like to do a great service for
your country . . . desert!**

It's an eyesight testing chart for the regulating branch!

It's been a terrible day RPO, nobody's done a thing wrong!

**Chef, I'll never forget the taste of your
Cornish pasties . . . no matter how hard I try!**

I told my mum I'd been made Ordinary Seaman. She says, "Be kind to your men"!

Diver Dingle located a mine sir, as a matter of fact he fell down it!

Take the book in your right hand and repeat after me . . . .

**Right lads, today we do a fifty mile route march,
a simulated air drop, twice round the Assault course,
followed by a couple of hours at the Rifle Range . . . then
after breakfast . . .**

That's still no excuse for being over 3 minutes & 43 seconds adrift!

Right, try it now sir!

Keei hauling at 1430, flogging at 1500, yard arm hanging
at 1630, plankwalking at 1700, . . . they should sack that
- - - - - entertainment's officer!

I can't estimate your efficiency in rating Grondle, it only
goes down as far as "bad"!

How sweet, a get well card from all the ship's galley staff!

I like everyone to see my dog-collar!

Tell the engine room to stop making black smoke. Green is much prettier!

That's just it, I have taken my flippers off!

Message from Mohawk sir!

**So you served on the Ark . . . you must be
fond of animals!**

No, I can't tell you what it is . . . I'm bound by the Official Secrets Act!

Hello skin . . . how was Porton Down!

Some game of uckers — they're playing injury time!

Permission to smoke sir?

They say he spent 5 years in a Japanese Prisoner of War camp . . . as the Commandant!

It must be your cooking Chef, any other ship would have
SEAGULLS round it's gash-shute!

I need cheering up No 1 . . . let's have Divisions.

**When my time comes, I want my ashes scattered . . . all
over the Wardroom carpet!**

But Master, the First Lieutenant gave me permission to bring a cat on board.

No 1, I think the Navigating Officer is trying to work his ticket.

The ship's company enjoyed your faggots, don't spoil it by telling them you trapped your hand in the mincing machine!

I've been ordered to leave you here . . . they can't afford
your back pay!

It's no use No 1, I still don't like the colour!

**These things can land anywhere.
This one's got 6 parking tickets.**

Now that's what I call REAL seamanship . . . eating a plate of your Spaghetti Bolognese in a Force 12 gale!

48

It's from my mum, it says Dear Son, Thanks for
the parrot, it was delicious!

No, they don't have jaunties on Submarines . . . how did you guess!

Yes sir you could eat off my galley floor, and that's what you'll be doing if this weather keeps up!

Yes mummy, I do miss him . . . as often as possible!

I was courting the daughter of the Drafting Commander, he hated me . . . what's your reason for being here!

I'll murder that Quartermaster who piped "Hands to Bathe" in dry dock!

**He has scrambled egg on his cap, fruit salad on his chest
and soup stains on his tie!**

**My old man used to keep two boozers . . . me &
me brother!**

I'd have you flogged __ if I thought I could get anything for you!

**Guess what . . . I found an English coin in the collection
this morning!**

**Me & your father served together in the old Ironduke . . .
Him behind the bar, me collecting in the empties!**

**I told you I would do well in the Navy. They've named
a disease after me!**

How do you expect me to ring eight bells, there's only one here!

Dive! Dive! Dive! . . . the wife and her mother are waiting to welcome me on the jetty!

It's great to be back on dry land!

No, nothing to declare!

The first thing she'll say when I get home is . . . when are you goin' back!

Of course it's genuine fur, it had to go into quarantine for
six months.

Displacement 7½ lbs. Length 14″ - Breadth 5½″ Power unit functioning normally . . . . .

Get the washing machine ready Dear, I've brought my overalls!

Of course it was necessary to buy two! One talks and the other translates what he says into English!

I had no chance to buy presents, Nuclear Subs go around the world . . . underwater!

Of course I wrote regularly . . . didn't you get them
bottles I tossed overboard in Mid-Pacific!

**So you've just completed your annual fortnight's
exercise . . . you didn't lose much weight!**

How romantic . . . you travel 25,000 miles, see 40 different countries, you're away 2 years, and all you bring me are 2 cases of dirty washing!

Right, you can take that lot back!

Alright, if you really insist, I'll put some salt in the water!

**PLEASE, when you go back off your leave,
take me with you!**

It'll take more than an afternoon off to bury my mother-in-law, I haven't even bought a spade yet!

Cut down on the Duty Frees — you're coughing up soot!

The wife wants to know when I'm coming on leave again . . . she wants to go out!

**You're tellin' me the Marines are always in first mate . . .
first in the dinner queue, first in the Liberty boat, first in
the Pub . . . first . . . . .**

**They're my husbands trophies, he was a member of the
Field Gun Crew!**

Don't get up when the Admiral does his round . . . just lay to attention!

**I couldn't return from an expensive fishing holiday
with nothing!**

I joined for the travel, sport, uniform and comradeship . . . and as an alternative to life imprisonment!

Right, disconnect the jackstay . . . the Padre's going to walk across!

I want to start my own business in Civvy Street, if I can find a nice little Borstal going cheap!

You should join the Navy son . . . it'll make a man of you!

**Why shouldn't I go to sea, I can be sick as good
as you can!**

**No, I won't kiss you Goodnight, but I will
kiss you Goodbye!**

Let's see, one egg 3 minutes, so that's
30 eggs, 90 minutes!

Buzz off Jack, we don't play requests!

We've found traces of blood in your alcohol!

.. and when you die do you want to be buried, cremated
or framed?

**Look, I've tried to see the Boss about a rise . . .
the Guards wouldn't let me in the Palace!**

Could you take a photo of me & my little boy - Jack?

I could offer you a job — have you got any references?